The Ultimate

Air Fryer Cookbook

Full-Coloured Book with Delicious Family Meals Easy to Prepare

Lilly Knight

TABLE OF CONTENTS

INTRODUCTION

Air Fryers have started to become popular, due to the fact that you can avoid many of the unhealthy aspects of modern cooking. But what is an Air Fryer exactly, and how on earth does it work?

Air Fryers are basically an upgraded, enhanced countertop oven, but they became popular for one particular reason. In fact, many of the manufacturers, such as Philips, market this machine solely based on the claim that the Air Fryers accurately mimic deep-frying, which, although extremely unhealthy, is still very popular in this day and age (as it is, in my opinion, one of the most delicious ways to eat food).

Air Fryers work with the use of a fan and a heating mechanism. You place the food you want cooked in a basket or on the rack, turn on the machine, and the Air Fryer distributes oven-temperature hot air around your food. It provides consistent, pervasive heat evenly to all the food within. This heat circulation achieves the crispy taste and texture that is so tantalizing in deep fried foods, but without the unhealthy and dangerous oil! Both have been replaced by this miracle machine with hot air and a fan.

ADVANTAGES TO USING AN AIR FRYER

I may have already slipped in a few of the advantages to using an Air Fryer, but now let's expand a little more on everything an Air Fryer can do for you. After all, no investment should be made unless it's absolutely worthwhile.

And in truth, the Air Fryer is very worthwhile. I cannot begin to tell you how the advantages start piling up; this is not just another average appliance that everyone is getting because of a simple trend. People are getting Air Fryers because of their incredible, numerous, multifaceted benefits.

There are, however, a few notable advantages of using an Air Fryer, which I'll list below. If you don't know anything else about Air Fryers, I hope that these will convince you of their worth.

HEALTHIER COOKING

This is perhaps the top benefit that comes with air frying. In a society that really struggles with healthy cooking, we can use all the help we can get. Luckily, Air Fryers make it easy, all while maintaining many of the factors that make unhealthy food delicious!
Air Fryers use very little oil, which is one of the best ways to replace those unhealthy fried foods, like fried chicken, potatoes, and so many others. If you are like me (a lover of deep fried foods)

then this is the answer to your dilemma of healthy eating while still enjoying the crispy taste of food!

Do keep in mind that you still need to spray fried foods, such as fish, with a touch of oil to make sure it does get evenly crispy. All in all, however, there is no denying the amount of oils is a whole lot less.

This singular change makes all the difference in the world. Healthy eating has never been easier, as you'll get the same crispy and flavoursome results, with minimal amounts of added oils. You'll even be able to "fry" foods you never were able to before—the possibilities are endless!

SAFER AND EASIER

Nothing scares me more than a hot pot of oil. It is an accident waiting to happen, and getting struck with burning oil splatters is no joke! But this, and its corresponding injuries, is often the price to pay for deep fried foods.

Air Fryers are also user-friendly, and this makes a huge difference. You don't have to feel like you are studying for a degree when working with an Air Fryer. Making dinner is far less complicated in an Air Fryer than many of the traditional methods of cooking. For some meals—unless you choose one of the more complex recipes I'll share later—you can even revert to placing a small piece of meat (even if it happens to be frozen!) into the basket and select the cooking settings.

The simplicity of the Air Fryer is its beauty. You will save countless time and unnecessary frustrations, and still make delicious food!

FASTER THAN COOKING IN THE OVEN

Once you buy an Air Fryer and set it to heat for the first time, you won't know what hit you! The average normal oven needs about 10 minutes to preheat. Due to the Air Fryer's smaller size and innovative design, it will be ready to go in no time!

It's even faster during the actual cooking. With the circulation that allows your food to be cooked crisp and even, it cuts a whole lot of cooking time out of the equation. This is amazing, especially in this day and age where technology, work, friends, family, and even pets are constantly demanding our attention.

Just imagine! You could set your food in the Air Fryer, and (with some recipes) it will be ready to eat in less than 20 minutes!

SAVES SPACE

If you are someone living in a small apartment, or a student accommodation, then an Air Fryer is perfect for you. Air Fryers are much smaller in comparison to a conventional oven and you can easily make use of this Air Fryer in 1 cubic foot of your kitchen.

You can even pack your Air Fryer away after use if need be, but the majority of people choose to keep it out on the counter. But it's nice to have the option to move your Air Fryer around if space becomes an issue.

LOW OPERATING COSTS

Considering how much cooking oil costs these days and the amount you need to use, you will soon be cutting costs in making deep fried foods. All an Air Fryer uses is a small amount of oil and some of the electricity to power up the Air Fryer, about the same amount that a countertop oven would.

Not only will you be cutting out the massive oil costs, which will save money, you will likely also save money by ordering out less, as you'll be able to replicate your favourite foods quickly and easily at home!

NO OIL SMELL

In reality, smelling like the food you just ate is not impressive, regardless of how delicious the food may be. This is what often happens, however, when people enjoy deep fried foods.

When deep frying foods, it also causes the whole house to smell, and as the oil splatters around, it can leave a massive mess. The oil can even harden on the walls, causing grime to build up into a nasty concentration of dirt and grease.

With less cooking oil, Air Fryers don't have any of those oil smells and keeps the space cleaner around you, as all the oils, smells, and actual cooking are contained within the machine.

PRESERVES NUTRIENTS

When you are cooking your food in an Air Fryer, it actually protects a lot of the food from losing all its moisture. This means that with the use of a little oil, as well as circulation with hot air, it can allow your food to keep most of its nutrients which is excellent for you!

If you want to cook healthy foods with the purpose of maintaining as many nutrients as possible, then an Air Fryer is perfect for you!

EASIER TO CLEAN

Cleaning is perhaps the bane of my existence, especially after cooking and having a long day. This can really take away a lot of the pleasure of making yourself a great meal. But an Air Fryer lightens the burden by being easy to clean!

Consistent cleaning after using it (much like any pot or pan) can allow for easier and simpler living. You just need some soapy water and a non-scratch sponge to clean both the exterior and the interior of your Air Fryer. Some Air Fryers are even dishwasher-safe!

GREAT FLAVOUR

The flavour of Air Fryer "fried" foods is nearly identical to traditional frying, and the texture is exact. You can cook a lot of those great frozen foods, such as onion rings or french fries, and still achieve that crunchy effect. This certainly can help you turn to healthier foods, especially if your goal is for healthy but quality meals.

The Air Fryer helps to cook your food to perfect crispness, instead of the soggy mess that happens when you try alternative methods of cooking foods that are meant to be deep fried (like chicken tenders). No one really enjoys mushy food. The Air Fryer keeps that desired element while remaining healthy.

All you will really need is just some cooking oil sprayed outside of your food to end up with a cooked interior and a crunchy exterior. So no worries! You still can eat your foods with a crunch and a healthier result!

VERSATILE

Unlike rice cookers meant just for rice, or bread makers meant just for bread, you will find that an Air Fryer leaves a lot of room to be both versatile and healthier. You can cook almost anything you would like in the Air Fryer (as long as it fits). From spaghetti squash, to desserts, even to fried chicken!
You will probably never run out of air frying options!

VARIOUS TYPES OF AIR FRYERS AND HOW TO CHOOSE THE ONE FOR YOU

There isn't one standardized choice of Air Fryers, which means you are far more likely to find an Air Fryer that really suits your particular needs. Whether it be size or price, you have a wider variety of choices than what normally comes with conventional ovens.

So what are the key aspects that you need to take into consideration when getting yourself a nice Air Fryer? Let's begin:

- **Dimensions:** Obviously they come in different sizes, and despite saving space, some can still be bulky. When thinking about your countertop, you do want to consider its size and dimensions. You don't want to play a game of tilt with your Air Fryer, nor have it taken up all the extra space you have!

- **Safety Features:** You may want to check that it has an auto shutoff, as it is certainly a desirable feature. Air Fryers can get very hot during use, and an auto-shutoff can save you a lot of stress and fire emergencies. Furthermore, having a cool exterior can prevent potential red and burnt hands. So do yourself a favour and make sure they have all these elements at hand.

- **Reviews:** Naturally, this is the best thing to check out. Considering that the businesses rarely give out all the information, you will certainly find it out when people leave reviews. The customer hides nothing, and if they are unhappy, they make sure everyone else knows about it. However, if people are very happy, many of them will also note it in the reviews, and it is best to target the Air Fryers that tend to have the high reviews.

TWO COMMON DIFFERENCES

Beyond those functional differences, there are two mainstream designs of Air Fryers: basket Air Fryers and oven Air Fryers. Each has very unique and distinguished features in which to enjoy. Let us take a look at the differences between the two:

BASKET AIR FRYERS

Basket fryers are known to need less space than oven Air Fryers, which is very practical if you have limited space. Not only does it save space, but it also saves time, as the food is quickly heated up (without unnecessarily heating up the kitchen). Unlike an oven Air Fryer, and the larger traditional oven, it only takes about 1-2 minutes for the basket Air Fryer to heat up, and it is quite easy to place the foods inside of the basket.

The cons are, for one, that it does make a lot more noise than the oven Air Fryer. You also will not be able to watch the food as it cooks, which can increase the chances of burnt food if you are not careful. Also, a basket Air Fryer may not be the best if you need to cook a lot of food, as it is limited in capacity. This means that batch cooking may be required if you need a large amount of food.

This makes a basket Air Fryer ideal if you have a limited budget, don't need to cook a huge amount of food, and have limited free time. They are quick, small, and convenient, especially perfect for people who are students or single working professionals, and maybe even you!

OVEN AIR FRYERS

Oven Air Fryers, in contrast, have a larger capacity, which means you can cook a lot more food at the same time. They also have multiple functions for cooking and cut down on the noise than the basket Air Fryer. You will also be able to move the food closer or even further away from the heating element. There is a lot more flexibility involved in the use of an oven Air Fryer. Best of all, you can place parts of the oven Air Fryer into the dishwasher to be washed (thus cutting down the cleaning process, if you happen to have a dishwasher).

But, do be aware that it takes up more counter space, and takes a larger initial bite out of your wallet. It may also heat up the kitchen more, and if you are in fashion and aesthetic design, it might be disappointing to find out the colours and themes are more limited than basket Air Fryers.

These are the two main common types of Air Fryers; however, there are new types of Air Fryers that are coming to light for you to use and enjoy, most notably, the paddle-type Air Fryer. This version has a paddle that moves through the basket of your Air Fryer in order to help circulate hot air in between each piece of food.

This saves you the effort of pulling your food out at a specific time and shaking or stirring it. These can also be noisy, and heat up the space, and are not small and convenient; however, if you are someone looking for convenience, then this is the Air Fryer to go for.

ACCESSORY TOOLS FOR AIR FRYER COOKING

I love how Air Fryers save time, so I've compiled a list of my favorite time-saving tools that I often use when meal prepping with my Air Fryer. Anything to help make your life easier and healthier should certainly be considered, and what better way to help than by adding some accessories to your Air Fryer inventory?

MANDOLINE

Preparation is always needed before jumping into air frying, and getting yourself the mandoline slicer is the perfect tool to slice online rings, pickles, or even the best and crunchiest chips. You can select the thickness or thinness, depending on what the recipe needs and says, so you will always be able to get the perfect crispness.

GRILL PAN

This is simply a pan created with a perforated surface. With this tool, you can both grill and sear foods like fish or even vegetables inside your Air Fryer. They are also commonly non-stick, which really helps your overall cleanup.

However, before you purchase a grill pan, make sure the Air Fryer model you have does support the grill pan. The last thing you want is to find that your grill pan just does not fit inside your Air Fryer.

HEAT RESISTANT TONGS

There is no denying how hot an Air Fryer can get inside, and unless you are a superhero, you will need some help manoeuvring in foods in and outside of the basket if need be. Using heat-resistant tongs can really make your life infinitely easier by keeping your foods, and your hands, safe. They are affordable, and really useful to allow for an even cooking process.

AIR FRYER LINERS

If you'd like to further decrease your clean-up time, then this is for you! These liners are both non-stick and non-toxic, making this a classic little investment for you to consider. They prevent the food from sticking to your Air Fryer and help in the process of keeping your little machine clean. You will not have to worry about burnt foods inside your fryer again!

AIR FRYER RACK

This adds a little bit more versatility as you can really take advantage of the surface cooking. With a rack, you ensure that heat is evenly distributed to all 360 degrees of your food. They are very safe and easy to use, and they increase the number of dishes you can cook at the same time

BAKING PANS

With an Air Fryer, you can even bake! You just need the right equipment, such as a barrel or round pan. With this you can even bake pizza, bread, muffins, and more. Imagine telling people you baked your own cake with an Air Fryer!

SILICONE BAKING CUPS

From egg bites to muffins, these are individual cups you can use in order to help compensate for the smaller space within an Air Fryer. The silicone material is heat-resistant, and allows for easier release of the contents, which spares you a lot of time cleaning. If you are a fan of baking, then this is a must have.

OIL SPRAYER

Naturally, one of the top benefits is needing much less oil when cooking with an Air Fryer, but it does not necessarily mean that you can cook with no oil at all. An oil sprayer is the key to getting the food you want to that nice golden-brown. You can use any oil that you like to use when cooking; all you need is a little spritz before you close the machine, and you are set!

THERMAPEN

Having the right cooking time is very important, but temperature also counts for a lot, and this is a nice little accessory to add to your collection. Having an instant-read thermometer can ensure all the food you have is cooked (and evenly so). If you are not completely certain at what temperatures food should be, you can always check out the various different guides.

HOW TO CLEAN AN AIR FRYER

As mentioned before, an Air Fryer is really easy to clean, but that doesn't mean you'll never need to clean it! Also, please remember that the cleanliness of your machine depends on how often you use it, and what you use it for.

It is recommended that you clean your Air Fryer after every use. As tempting as it may be to skip a day, it really is not worth it over the long run.
And that is the first step that comes with cleaning an Air Fryer:

- Do not delay the cleaning. Simply don't. Allowing crumbs or random bits of food to harden overnight can turn an easy task into a nightmare of a chore. If you do happen to air-fry foods that come with a form of sticky sauce, then the warmer they are, the easier again they will be to clean and remove.

- Unplug the machine, and use warm and soapy water to properly remove the dirt and components. You do not want anything abrasive in there. If there is food that gets stuck, try soaking it until it is soft enough to remove.

- If there is any food that happens to be stuck on the grate or in the basket, then you should consider gently using a toothpick or even a wooden skewer to scrape it off, in order to be thorough with your cleaning process.

- Remember to wipe the inside with a damp, soapy cloth, and remember to remove both the drawer and the basket.

- Finally, wipe the outside of your Air Fryer with a damp cloth or a sponge.

If there are any odors that seem to be stuck to your Air Fryer after cooking a strong food, even after you have cleaned it, then you can consider using a product called NewAir.

Just soak it in with water for about 30 minutes to an hour before you clean it. If the smell remains, then rub one lemon half over the drawer and the basket. Allow it to soak for another 30 minutes before washing it again.

Please do be careful with any non-stick appliances. They are a wonder for cleaning, but they can flake or come off over time. Be gentle, as you do not want anything to scratch or to even chip the coating. Not only does it ruin a little bit of the aesthetic look, a small part of your Air Fryer will constantly be struggling with sticky food.

There you have it! The first stepping stones and foundational knowledge of an Air Fryer. The device you will choose, and how you will use it is up to you, but there are still so many exciting varieties, choices, and options to come!

CHAPTER 1: BREAKFAST RECIPES

LEMON-BLUEBERRY MUFFINS

5 minutes

25 minutes

6

INGREDIENTS

- 350 g almond flour
- 3 tbsp Swerve Sweetener
- 1tsp baking powder
- 2 large eggs
- 3 tbsp melted butter
- 1tbsp almond milk
- 1 tbsp fresh lemon juice
- 65 g fresh blueberries

DIRECTIONS

1. Preheat the air fryer to 177°C (350°F). Lightly coat 6 silicone muffin cups with vegetable oil. Set aside.
2. Mix the almond flour, Swerve, and baking soda in a bowl. Set aside.
3. Mix the eggs, butter, milk, and lemon juice in a separate bowl. Combine the egg mixture with the flour mixture and stir until just combined. Roll in the blueberries and let the batter sit for 5 min.
4. Set the muffin batter into the muffin cups, about two-thirds full. Air fry for 20 to 25 min, or until a toothpick inserted into the centre of a muffin comes out clean.
5. Detach the basket from the device and let the muffins cool for about 5 min.

Nutrition: Calories: 165; Fat: 11g; Carbs: 8g; Net Carbs: 7g; Fibre: 1g

SCOTCH EGGS

15 minutes

12 minutes

6

INGREDIENTS

- 6 boiled eggs peeled
- 1 packet 400g Powters Sausagemeat
- 30 g Flour
- ½ teaspoon garlic powder
- 1 large egg beaten
- 120 g Breadcrumbs
- 1 tablespoon brown sugar
- ½ smoked paprika

DIRECTIONS

1. Divide the sausage into 6 equal portions and roll them into a balls
2. Place a sausage ball on your counter or parchment paper if you don't want to clean up later.
3. Pat the sausage balls until they reach the form of an oval big enough to hold an egg.
4. Place the peeled, boiled eggs in the center of the sausages patties and wrap the sausages around the eggs, applying pressure with your hands.
5. Now take 3 bowls and put, in order: flour and garlic powder combined, beaten egg, panko or breadcrumbs with brown sugar and smoked paprika.
6. Roll each sausage-covered egg in bowl 1, then dip in bowl 2 and coat in the breadcrumbs bowl.
7. Preheat your air fryer to 190°C for 10 minutes.
8. Place Scotch eggs in the air fryer basket, ensuring enough space between each other to let the air circulate.
9. Air fry the eggs for 12 minutes, evenly turning halfway through to brown.

Nutrition: Calories 396; Fat 27 g; Protein 29 g; Carbs 16 g; Fibre 1 g; Sugar 1 g

WALNUT PANCAKE

10 minutes

20 minutes

4

INGREDIENTS

- 3 tbsp melted butter, divided
- 130 g flour
- 2 tbsp sugar
- 1½ tsp baking powder
- ¼ tsp salt
- 1 egg, beaten
- 95 ml milk
- 1 tsp pure vanilla extract
- 65 g roughly chopped walnuts
- Maple syrup or fresh sliced fruit, for serving

DIRECTIONS

1. Grease a baking pan with 1 tbsp of melted butter.
2. Mix together the flour, sugar, baking powder, and salt in a medium bowl. Add the beaten egg, the remaining 2 tbsp of melted butter, milk, and vanilla and stir until the batter is sticky but slightly lumpy.
3. Slowly pour the batter into the greased baking pan and scatter with the walnuts.
4. Place the pan on the bake position.
5. Select Bake, set temperature to 166°C (330°F), and set time to 20 min.
6. When cooked, the pancake should be golden brown and well cooked.
7. Let the pancake rest for 5 min and serve topped with maple syrup or fresh fruit, if desired.

Nutrition: Calories 271; Fat 14.5 g; Carbohydrates 22 g; Sugar 1.2 g; Protein 11 g

AIR FRYER BLACK PUDDING (PACKED)

0 minutes

9 minutes

2

INGREDIENTS

- Black Pudding Slices

DIRECTIONS

1. If your black pudding is still frozen, air fry it in the air fryer for 6 minutes at 80°C, then it will be soft enough to cut.
2. Remove from the air fryer. Cut into slices, removing the wrapper.
3. Place the slices in the frying basket and cook at 180°C for 9 minutes.
4. Serve.

Nutrition: Calories: 297kcal; Fat: 22 g

AIR FRIED TOMATO BREAKFAST QUICHE

10 minutes

30 minutes

1

INGREDIENTS

- 2 tbsp yellow onion, chopped
- 2 eggs
- 30 ml milk
- 65 g gouda cheese, shredded
- 30 g tomatoes, chopped
- Salt and black pepper to the taste
- Cooking Spray

DIRECTIONS

1. Set an air fryer pan with cooking spray.
2. Crack eggs, add onion, milk, cheese, tomatoes, salt and pepper and stir.
3. Cook at 170°C (340°F) for 30 min.
4. Serve hot and enjoy!

Nutrition: Calories 239; Fat 6.2; Fibre 8; Carbs 14; Protein 6

SAUSAGE AND CHEESE BALLS

12 minutes

12 minutes

16

INGREDIENTS

- 450 g pork breakfast sausage
- 65 g shredded Cheddar cheese
- 30 g full-fat cream cheese, softened
- 1 large egg

DIRECTIONS

1. Mix all ingredients in a large bowl. Form into sixteen (2.5 cm) balls. Move the balls into the air fryer basket.
2. Set the temperature to 200°C (400°F) and air fry for 12 min.
3. Shake the basket two- or three times during cooking. Sausage balls will now be browned on the outside and have an internal temperature of at least 63°C (145°F) when thoroughly cooked.
4. Serve warm.

Nutrition: Calories: 424; Fat: 32g; Protein: 23g; Carbs: 2g; Fibre: 0g

BACON-AND-EGGS AVOCADO

5 minutes	17 minutes	1

INGREDIENTS

- 1 large egg
- 1 avocado, halved, peeled, and pitted
- Bacon slices
- Fresh parsley, for serving (optional)
- Sea salt flakes, for garnish (optional)

DIRECTIONS

1. Set the air fryer basket with avocado oil. Preheat the air fryer to 160°C (320°F). Fill a small bowl with cool water.
2. Soft boil the egg: Place the egg in the air fryer basket. Air fry for 6 min for a soft yolk or 7 min for a cooked yolk. Put the egg in the bowl of cool water and let it sit for 2 min. Peel and set aside.
3. Use a spoon to carve out extra space in the centre of the avocado halves until the cavities are big enough to fit the soft-boiled egg. Place the soft-boiled egg in the centre of one half of the avocado and replace the other half of the avocado on top, so the avocado appears whole on the outside.
4. Starting at one end of the avocado, wrap the bacon around the avocado to completely cover it.
5. Place the bacon-wrapped avocado in the air fryer basket and air fry for 5 min. Flip the avocado over and air fry for another 5 min or until the bacon is cooked to your liking. If desired, serve on a bed of fresh parsley, and sprinkle with salt flakes.
6. Best served fresh.

Nutrition: Calories: 536; Fat: 46g; Protein: 18g; Carbs: 18g; Fibre: 14g

NUTTY GRANOLA

5 minutes

45 minutes

4

INGREDIENTS

- 65 g pecans, coarsely chopped
- 65 g walnuts or almonds, chopped
- 30 g unsweetened flaked coconut
- 30 g almond flour
- 30 g flaxseed or chia seeds
- 2 tbsp sunflower seeds
- 2 tbsp melted butter
- 30 g Swerve
- 1/2 tsp ground cinnamon
- 1/2 tsp vanilla extract
- 1/4 tsp ground nutmeg
- 1/4 tsp salt
- 2 tbsp water

DIRECTIONS

1. Preheat the air fryer to 120°C (250°F). Divide a piece of parchment paper to fit inside the air fryer basket.
2. In a large bowl, toss all the ingredients until thoroughly combined.
3. Spread now the granola on the parchment paper and flatten to an even thickness.
4. Air fry for 45 min, or until golden throughout. Detach from the air fryer and allow to fully cool. Now break the granola into bite-size pieces and store in a covered container for up to a week.

Nutrition: Calories: 305; Fat: 28g; Protein: 8g; Carbs: 10g; Fibre: 6g

BLT BREAKFAST WRAP

5 minutes

10 minutes

4

INGREDIENTS

- 230 g bacon
- 8 tbsp mayonnaise
- 8 large romaine lettuce leaves
- 4 Roma tomatoes, sliced
- Salt and ground black pepper, to taste

DIRECTIONS

1. Set the bacon in a single layer in the air fryer basket. (It's OK if the bacon sits a bit on the sides.) Set the air fryer to 175°C (350°F) and air fry for 10 min. Cook in batches, if necessary, and drain the grease in between sets. Check for crispiness and air fry for 2 to 3 min longer if needed.
2. Scatter 1 tbsp of mayonnaise on each of the lettuce leaves and top with the tomatoes and cooked bacon. Flavour to taste with salt and freshly ground black pepper. Roll the lettuce leaves as you would a burrito, securing with a toothpick if desired.

Nutrition: Calories: 370; Fat: 34g; Protein: 11g Carbs: 7g; Fibre: 3g

YORKSHIRE PUDDINGS

| 1 hour | 18 minutes | 4 |

INGREDIENTS

- 1 egg
- 4 tbsp (70 g) flour
- 4 tbsp (80 ml) milk
- 4 tbsp (80 ml) water
- 1/4 tsp salt

DIRECTIONS

1. Mix well all the ingredients together; you need to obtain a smooth batter with no lumps
2. Once the batter is ready, refrigerate for 30 to 60 minutes
3. Preheat the air fryer to 200 C
4. Grease a ramekin with some butter, then add a tsp of oil; heat at 200C in the air fryer for five minutes. This operation will prevent the batter from sticking
5. Once the ramekins are hot, add five tablespoons of Yorkshire Pudding mixture to each one
6. Cook at 200 C for 18 minutes
7. Do not open the air fryer while cooking!

Nutrition: Calories 89; Fat 2 g; Protein 4 g; Carbs 13 g; Fibre 2 g; Sugar 1 g

CREAMY MASHED POTATOES

5 minutes

25 minutes

4

INGREDIENTS

- 900 baking potatoes (small to medium)
- 40 g butter
- 60 g cream cheese
- 2 stalks of fresh chives
- salt and pepper to taste

DIRECTIONS

1. Start by placing your potatoes into a foil packet, Layout your foil, then place the potatoes in them.
2. Air fry for 25 minutes at 200C. Check after 25 minutes if they are soft; The actual time will depend on the type of air fryer you have and the size of the potatoes.
3. Use a fork (or a potato masher if you prefer) to mash the potatoes.
4. Put the potatoes in a bowl.
5. Add the cream cheese and butter.
6. Add the chives and continue to mix. Continue mixing until the potatoes are mashed and the cream cheese and butter are combined.
7. Plate, serve and enjoy!

Nutrition: Calories: 322; Sugar: 3 g; Fat: 11 g; Carbohydrates: 50 g; Fibre: 5 g; Protein: 7 g

SIMPLE BALSAMIC-GLAZED CARROTS

5 minutes

18 minutes

3

INGREDIENTS

- 3 medium-size carrots, cut into 5 cm × 1.2 cm sticks
- 1 tbsp orange juice
- 2 tsps balsamic vinegar
- 1 tsp maple syrup
- 1 tsp avocado oil
- 1/2 tsp dried rosemary
- 1/4 tsp sea salt
- 1/4 tsp lemon zest

DIRECTIONS

1. Put the carrots in a baking pan and sprinkle with the balsamic vinegar, orange juice, maple syrup, avocado oil, sea salt, and rosemary, finishing with the lemon zest. Toss well.
2. Place the pan on the toast position.
3. Select Toast, set temperature to 200°C (392°F), and set time to 18 min. Stir the carrots several times during cooking.
4. When cooking is done, the carrots should be nicely glazed and tender.

Nutrition: Calories 113; Fat 4.7 g; Carbohydrates 17 g; Protein 1 g; Fibre 3.4 g; Sugar 10 g

ASPARAGUS AND GREEN BEANS SALAD

15 minutes   6 minutes   3

INGREDIENTS

- 85 g asparagus, chopped
- 60 g green beans, chopped
- 130 g arugula, chopped
- 1 tbsp hazelnuts, chopped
- 1 tsp flax seeds
- 60 g Mozzarella, chopped
- 1 tbsp olive oil
- ½ tsp salt
- ½ tsp ground paprika
- ½ tsp ground black pepper
- Cooking Spray

DIRECTIONS

1. Preheat the air fryer to 200°C (400°F). Put the asparagus and green beans in the air fryer and spray them with cooking spray. Cook the vegetables for 6 minutes at 200°C (400°F). Shake the vegetables after 3 minutes of cooking. Then cool them to room temperature and put them in the salad bowl.
2. Add hazelnuts, flax seeds, chopped Mozzarella, salt, ground paprika, and ground black pepper. Sprinkle the salad with olive oil and shake well.

Nutrition: Calories: 122; Fat: 9.4g; Fibre: 1.9g; Carbs: 4.3g; Protein:6.9g

MUSHROOM CAKES

10 minutes

8 minutes

4

INGREDIENTS

- 255 g mushrooms, finely chopped
- 30 g coconut flour
- 1 tsp salt
- 1 egg, beaten
- 85 g Cheddar cheese, shredded
- 1 tsp dried parsley
- ½ tsp ground black pepper
- 1 tsp sesame oil
- 30 g spring onion, chopped

DIRECTIONS

1. Preheat the air fryer to 200°C (385°F). Mix up chopped mushrooms, coconut flour, salt, egg, dried parsley, ground black pepper, and minced onion in the mixing bowl. Stir the mixture until smooth and add Cheddar cheese (stir it with the help of the fork). Line the air fryer pan with baking paper.
2. With the help of the spoon, make medium size patties and put them in the pan. Sprinkle the patties with sesame oil and cook for 4 minutes on each side.

Nutrition: Calories: 164; Fat: 10.7g; Fibre: 3.9g; Carbs: 7.8g; Protein:10.3g

MASHED POTATO PANCAKES

5 minutes

15 minutes

6

INGREDIENTS

- 250 g Mashed Potatoes
- 100 g cheddar cheese
- 1 green onion chopped
- 2 strips of cooked bacon
- 1 egg
- 2 tbsp flour
- 100 g panko bread crumbs
- Salt and Pepper to taste

DIRECTIONS

1. Mix Potatoes, egg, cheese,bacon, green onion, and flour
2. Make into a patty form.
3. Coat in panko bread crumbs
4. Place in the freezer for 10 minutes to hold form.
5. Place foil over your rack on your air fryer
6. Cook on 200 C for 10 minutes
7. Flip over and cook for an additional 5 minutes.

Nutrition: Calories: 273; Total Fat: 13g; Carbohydrates: 28g; Fibre: 2g; Sugar: 2g; Protein: 11g

COURGETTE AND POTATO TOTS

5 minutes

20 minutes

4

INGREDIENTS

- 1 large courgette, grated
- 1 medium baked potato, skin removed and mashed
- 30 g shredded Cheddar cheese
- 1 large egg, beaten
- 1/2 tsp kosher salt
- Cooking Spray

DIRECTIONS

1. Place the baking pan on the air fry position. Select Air Fry, set the temperature to 199°C (390°F), and set the time to 10 min.
2. Wrap now the grated courgette in a paper towel and squeeze out any excess liquid, then combine the courgette, baked potato, shredded Cheddar cheese, egg, and kosher salt in a large bowl.
3. Spray the baking pan with cooking spray, then place individual tablespoons of the courgette mixture in the pan. Air fry for 10 min. Repeat this process with the remaining mixture.
4. Remove the tots and allow to cool on a wire rack for 5 min before serving.

Nutrition: Calories 128; Fat 3.5 g; Carbohydrates 17 g; Protein 5.3 g; Fibre 2 g; Sugar 1.5 g

BRUSSELS SPROUTS IN AIR FRYER

20 minutes

5 minutes

5

INGREDIENTS

- 1/4 tsp. salt
- 1 tbsp. balsamic vinegar
- 1 tbsp. olive oil
- 400 g Brussels sprouts

DIRECTIONS

1. Cut Brussels sprouts in half lengthwise. Toss with salt, vinegar, and olive oil till coated thoroughly.
2. Add coated sprouts to air fryer, cooking 8-10 min at 200°C (400°F). Shake after 5 min of cooking.
3. Brussels sprouts are ready to devour when brown and crisp!

Nutrition: Calories 430; Fat 26.5 g; Carbohydrates 27.1 g; Sugar 0 g; Protein 16.7 g

LEMON AND BUTTER ARTICHOKE

5 minutes

15 minutes

4

INGREDIENTS

- 340 g artichoke hearts
- Juice of ½ lemon
- 4 tbsp butter, melted
- 2 tbsp tarragon, chopped
- Salt and black pepper to the taste

DIRECTIONS

1. In a bowl, mix all the ingredients, toss, transfer the artichokes to your air fryer's basket and cook at 188°C (370°F) for 15 minutes.
2. Prepare the portions and serve them as a side dish.

Nutrition: Calories: 200; Fat: 7g; Fibre: 2g; Carbs: 3g; Protein:7 g

GOAT CHEESE CAULIFLOWER AND BACON

 5 minutes

 20 minutes

 4

INGREDIENTS

- 1 Kg cauliflower florets, roughly chopped
- 4 bacon strips, chopped
- Salt and black pepper to the taste
- 65 g spring onions, chopped
- 1 tbsp garlic, minced
- 285 g goat cheese, crumbled
- 30 g soft cream cheese
- Cooking Spray

DIRECTIONS

1. Grease a baking pan that fits the air fryer with the cooking spray and mix all the ingredients except the goat cheese into the pan.
2. Sprinkle the cheese on top, introduce the pan to the air fryer and cook at 200°C (400°F) for 20 minutes. Prepare the portions and serve them as a side dish.

Nutrition: Calories: 203; Fat: 13g; Fibre: 2g; Carbs: 5g; Protein:9g

CRISPY CHEESY ASPARAGUS

15 minutes

6 minutes

4

INGREDIENTS

- 2 egg whites
- 30 ml water
- 30 g + 2 tbsp of grated Parmesan cheese, divided
- 90 g panko breadcrumbs
- 1⁄4 tsp salt
- 340 g of fresh asparagus spears, ends trimmed
- Cooking Spray

DIRECTIONS

1. In a shallow dish, whisk together egg whites, water, until slightly foamy. Thoroughly combine 32 g of Parmesan cheese, breadcrumbs, and salt in a separate shallow dish.
2. Dip now the asparagus in the egg white, then roll in the cheese mixture to coat well.
3. Place the asparagus in the air fry basket in a single layer, leaving space between each spear. Spritz the asparagus with cooking spray.
4. Place the basket in the air fry position.
5. Select Air Fry, set the temperature to 199°C (390°F), and set the time to 6 min.
6. When cooking is done, the asparagus should be golden brown and crisp. Remove the basket from the air fryer grill. Sprinkle with the remaining 2 tbsp of cheese and serve hot.

Nutrition: Calories 130; Fat 1.3 g; Carbohydrates 22 g; Protein 6.8 g; Fibre 2.5 g; Sugar 3 g

LEMON-PEPPER CHICKEN WINGS

10-30 minutes

24 minutes

10

INGREDIENTS

- 900 g chicken wing flats and drumettes (about 16 to 20 pieces)
- 1.1⁄2 tsps kosher salt or 3⁄4 tsp fine salt
- 1.1⁄2 tsps baking powder
- 4.1⁄2 tsps salt-free lemon pepper seasoning

DIRECTIONS

1. Place the wings in a large bowl.
2. In a tiny bowl, stir the salt, baking powder, and seasoning mix. Sprinkle now the mixture over the wings and toss thoroughly to coat the wings. (This works best with your hands.) If you have time, let the wings sit for 20 to 30 min. Place the wings in the baking pan, ensuring they don't touch each other too much.
3. Place the pan on the air fry position. Select Air Fry, set the temperature to 190°C (375°F), and set the time to 24 min.
4. After twelve min, remove the pan from the grill. Using tongs, turn the wings over. Rotate the pan at 180 degrees and return the pan to the grill to continue cooking.
5. When cooking is done, the wings should be dark golden brown and a bit charred in places. Remove the pan, and let cool before serving.

Nutrition: Calories 171; Fat 11.5 g; Carbohydrates 1.2 g; Protein 15.7 g; Fibre 0 g; Sugar 0 g

SWEET AND SPICY TURKEY MEATBALLS

15 minutes

15 minutes

6

INGREDIENTS

- 450 g lean ground turkey
- 65 g whole-wheat panko breadcrumbs
- 1 egg, beaten
- 1 tbsp soy sauce
- 30 g plus 1 tbsp hoisin sauce, divided
- 2 tsps minced garlic
- 1/8 tsp salt
- 1/8 tsp freshly ground black pepper
- 1 tsp sriracha
- Olive oil spray

DIRECTIONS

1. Spray the crisper tray lightly with olive oil spray.
2. Place the crisper tray on the air fry position. Select Air Fry, set temp to 175°C (350°F), and set the time to 15 min.
3. Mix the turkey, panko breadcrumbs, egg, soy sauce, 1 tbsp of hoisin sauce, garlic, salt, and black pepper.
4. Using a tbsp, form the mixture into 24 meatballs.
5. In a small bowl, combine the remaining 30 g of hoisin sauce and sriracha to make a glaze and set aside.
6. Place the meatballs in the crisper tray in a single layer. You may need to cook them in batches.
7. Air fry for 8 min. Brush now the meatballs generously with the glaze and air fry until cooked through, an additional 4 to 7 min.
8. Serve warm.

Nutrition: Calories 147; Fat 6 g; Carbohydrates 6.5 g; Protein 15 g; Fibre 0.3 g; Sugar 0.5 g

BAKED CHICKEN TENDERS

10 minutes

20 minutes

6-8

INGREDIENTS

- 450 g of boneless chicken tenders
- 2 eggs
- 2 tsp. of butter, melted
- 85 g of graham crackers
- 85 g of breadcrumbs
- Barbecue sauce
- Salt and pepper for seasoning

DIRECTIONS

1. Preheat the Air Fryer to 200°C (390°F) and spray some oil on the baking pan
2. Combine the crackers, breadcrumbs, and butter until smooth.
3. Beat the eggs in another bowl with salt and pepper.
4. Dip the chicken pieces in the eggs first and then the breadcrumbs.
5. Air fry for 15-18 min.

Nutrition: Calories 147; Fat 6 g; Carbohydrates 6 g; Protein 16.5 g; Fibre 0.2 g; Sugar 0.5 g

BACON-WRAPPED CHICKEN BREASTS

10 minutes   15 minutes   4

INGREDIENTS

- 30 g chopped fresh chives
- 2 tbsp lemon juice
- 1 tsp dried sage
- 1 tsp fresh rosemary leaves
- 65 g fresh parsley leaves
- 4 cloves garlic, peeled
- 1 tsp ground fennel
- 3 tsps. sea salt
- 1⁄2 tsp red pepper flakes
- 4 (115 g) skinless, boneless, chicken breasts, pounded 6.5 mm thick
- 8 slices bacon
- Sprigs of fresh rosemary, for garnish
- Cooking Spray

DIRECTIONS

1. Spritz the air fry basket with cooking spray.
2. Put the chives, garlic, fennel, salt, lemon juice, rosemary, parsley, sage, and red pepper flakes in a food processor, then pulse to purée until smooth.
3. Unfold the chicken breasts on a clean work surface, then brush the top side of the chicken breasts with the sauce.
4. Roll the chicken breasts up from the shorter side, then wrap each chicken roll with 2 bacon slices to cover. Secure with toothpicks.
5. Arrange the rolls in the air fry basket.
6. Place the basket on the air fry position.
7. Select Air Fry. Set temperature to 170°C (340°F) and set time to 10 min. Flip the rolls halfway through.
8. After 10 min, increase the temperature to 200°C (390°F) and set the time to 5 min.
9. When the cooking is done, the bacon should be browned and crispy.
10. Transfer the rolls to a large plate. Discard the toothpicks and spread with rosemary sprigs before serving.

Nutrition: Calories 221; Fat 11 g; Carbohydrates 1.25 g; Protein 31 g; Fibre 0.5 g; Sugar 0 g

ALMOND CHICKEN CURRY

10 minutes   15 minutes   2

INGREDIENTS

- 285 g chicken fillet, chopped
- 1 tsp ground turmeric
- 65 g spring onions, diced
- 1 tsp salt
- ½ tsp curry powder
- ½ tsp garlic, diced
- ½ tsp ground coriander
- 65 ml of organic almond milk
- 1 tsp Truvia
- 1 tsp olive oil

DIRECTIONS

1. Put the chicken in the bowl. Add the ground turmeric, salt, curry powder, diced garlic, coriander, and almond Truvia. Then add olive oil and mix up the chicken. After this, add almond milk and transfer the chicken in the air fryer pan. Then preheat the air fryer to 190°C(375°F) and place the pan with korma curry inside.
2. Top the chicken with diced onion.
3. Cook the meal for 10 minutes. Stir it after 5 minutes of cooking. If the chicken is not cooked after 10 minutes, cook it for an additional 5 minutes.

Nutrition: Calories: 327; Fat: 14.5 g; Fibre: 1.5 g; Carbs: 5.6 g; Protein:42 g

DELICIOUS CHICKEN FAJITAS

10 minutes

15 minutes

4

INGREDIENTS

- 4 chicken breasts
- 1 onion, sliced
- 1 bell pepper, sliced
- 1 1/2 tbsp. fajita seasoning
- 2 tbsp olive oil
- 95 g cheddar cheese, shredded

DIRECTIONS

1. Preheat the air fryer at 195°C (380°F).
2. Coat chicken with oil and rub it with seasoning.
3. Place chicken into the air fryer baking dish and top with bell peppers and onion.
4. Cook for 15 min.
5. Top with shredded cheese and cook for 1-2 min until cheese is melted.
6. Serve and enjoy.

Nutrition: Calories 425; Fat 23 g; Carbohydrates 7 g; Sugar 2 g; Protein 45 g

BBQ CHEDDAR STUFFED CHICKEN BREASTS

15 minutes

35 minutes

2

INGREDIENTS

- 3 strips bacon
- 2 (110 g) chicken breast skinless and boneless
- 60 g cheddar cheese, cubed
- 30 g BBQ sauce
- 1 pinch of salt and black pepper

DIRECTIONS

1. Place 1 strips of bacon in a crisper tray and air fry for 2 minutes. Cut the bacon into small pieces.
2. Line the crisper tray with parchment paper.
3. Make a horizontal 2.5 cm cut on the chicken to create an internal pouch.
4. Stuff each chicken breast with cooked bacon and cheese mixture, and then wrap the breasts with bacon.
5. Cover the chicken with BBQ sauce and place them on the lined tray.
6. Set the temperature of the Air Fryer to 195°C (380°F) and the time for 20 minutes.
7. Turn the chicken breasts halfway through cooking time. When fully cooked, the chicken's internal temperature should be 75°C (165°F). Serve.

Nutrition: Calories: 375; Fat: 19 g; Carbs: 12.3 g; Sugar: 0 g; Protein:38 g

TENDER SPICY CHICKEN

1-3 hours

20 minutes

4

INGREDIENTS

- 455 g chicken breasts, boneless, skinless
- 65 g rice wine
- 1 tbsp stone-ground mustard
- 1 tsp garlic, minced
- 1 tsp black peppercorns, whole
- 1 tsp chili powder
- 1/4 tsp of sea salt and more to taste

DIRECTIONS

1. Place the chicken, wine, mustard, garlic, and whole peppercorns in a ceramic bowl. Seal the bowl and let the chicken marinate as long as you can in your refrigerator (ideal for about 3 hours).
2. Discard the marinade and place the chicken breasts in the Air Fryer cooking basket.
3. Cook the chicken breasts at 195°C (380°F) for 12 min, turning them over halfway through the cooking time.
4. Season now the chicken with chili powder and salt. Serve immediately and enjoy!

Nutrition: Calories 404; Fat 29g; Carbohydrates 36g; Sugars 7g; Protein 24g

APPLE-GLAZED PORK

15 minutes	19 minutes	4

INGREDIENTS

- 1 sliced apple
- 1 small onion, sliced
- 2 tbsp apple cider vinegar, divided
- 1⁄2 tsp thyme
- 1⁄2 tsp rosemary
- 1⁄4 tsp brown sugar
- 3 tbsp olive oil, divided
- 1⁄4 tsp smoked paprika
- 4 pork chops
- Salt and ground black pepper, to taste

DIRECTIONS

1. Place the baking pan on the bake position. Select Bake, set the temperature to 177°C (350°F), and set the time to 4 min.
2. Combine the apple slices, onion, 1 tbsp of vinegar, thyme, rosemary, brown sugar, and 2 tbsp of olive oil in the baking pan. Stir to mix well.
3. Bake for 4 min.
4. Meanwhile, mix the remaining vinegar, olive oil, and paprika in a large bowl. Sprinkle with salt and ground black pepper. Stir to mix well. Dredge the pork in the mixture and toss to coat well.
5. Remove the baking pan from the grill and put in the pork. Air fry for 10 min to lightly brown the pork. Flip the pork chops halfway through.
6. Remove the pork from the grill and baste with baked apple mixture on both sides. Put the pork back to the grill and air fry for an additional 5 min. Flip halfway through.
7. Serve immediately.

Nutrition: Calories 531; Fat 33 g; Carbohydrates 5.5 g; Protein 41 g; Fibre 0.5 g; Sugar 4.3 g

EASY SPICY STEAKS WITH SALAD

15 minutes

15 minutes

4

INGREDIENTS

- 1 (680 g) boneless top sirloin steak, trimmed and halved crosswise
- 1.1/2 tsps chili powder
- 1.1/2 tsps ground cumin
- 3/4 tsp ground coriander
- 1/8 tsp cayenne pepper
- 1/8 tsp ground cinnamon
- 1.1/4 tsps plus 1/8 tsp salt, divided
- 1/2 tsp plus 1/8 tsp ground black pepper, divided
- 1 tsp plus 1 1/2 tbsp extra-virgin olive oil, divided
- 3 tbsp mayonnaise
- 1.1/2 tbsp white wine vinegar
- 1 tbsp minced fresh dill
- 1 small garlic clove, minced
- 230 g sugar snap peas, strings removed and cut in half on bias
- 1/2 English cucumber, halved lengthwise and sliced thin
- 2 radishes, trimmed, halved and sliced thin
- 255 g baby arugula

DIRECTIONS

1. In a bowl, mix coriander, cumin, cayenne pepper, chili powder, cinnamon, 1.1/4 tsps salt and 1/2 tsp pepper until well combined.
2. Add the steaks to another bowl and pat dry with paper towels. Brush with 1 tsp oil and transfer to the bowl of spice mixture. Roll over to coat thoroughly.
3. Arrange the coated steaks in the air fry basket, spaced evenly apart.
4. Place the basket in the air fry position.
5. Select Air Fry. Set temperature to 200°C (400°F) and set time to 15 min. Flip the steak halfway through to ensure even cooking.
6. When cooking is done, an instant-read thermometer inserted into the thickest part of the meat should register at least 63°C (145°F).
7. Transfer the steaks to a clean work surface and wrap with aluminium foil. Let stand while preparing salad.
8. To make the salad, stir together in a large bowl 1.1/2 tbsp of olive oil, vinegar, mayonnaise, dill, garlic, 1/8 tsp pepper, and 1/8 tsp salt. Add snap peas, cucumber, radishes and arugula. Toss to blend well.
9. Slice now the steaks and serve with the salad.

Nutrition: Calories 380; Fat 19 g; Carbohydrates 4 g; Protein 45 g; Fibre 1.2 g; Sugar 2 g

BEEF TENDERLOIN IN AIR FRYER

15 minutes

15 minutes

8

INGREDIENTS

- 900 g beef tenderloin
- 1 tbsp. vegetable oil
- 1 tbsp. dried oregano
- 1 tbsp. salt
- 1/2 tbsp. black pepper, cracked

DIRECTIONS

1. Pat dries tenderloin with paper towel and places it on a platter.
2. Drizzle vegetable oil and sprinkle oregano, salt, and pepper. Rub the spices on the meat until well coated.
3. Select the air fry setting. Set temperature at 200°C (390°F) for 22 min. Reduce now the temperature to 182°C (360°F) and cook for 10 min.
4. Set the meat to a plate and allow to rest while tented with paper foil for 10 min before serving.

Nutrition: Calories 235; Fat 10.6 g; Carbohydrates 0.2 g; Sugar 0 g; Protein 32.4 g

PANKO-CRUSTED LAMB RACK

10 minutes   20 minutes   2

INGREDIENTS

- 65 g finely chopped pistachios
- 1 tsp chopped fresh rosemary
- 3 tbsp panko breadcrumbs
- 2 tsps chopped fresh oregano
- 1 tbsp of olive oil
- Salt, freshly ground black pepper, to taste
- 1 lamb rack, bones fat trimmed, frenched
- 1 tbsp Dijon mustard

DIRECTIONS

1. Put the oregano, pistachios, rosemary, olive oil, breadcrumbs, salt, and black pepper in a food processor. Pulse to combine until smooth.
2. Rub now the lamb rack with the salt and the black pepper on a clean work surface, then place it in the air fry basket.
3. Place the basket in the air fry position.
4. Select Air Fry. Set temperature to 195°C (380°F) and set time to 12 min. Flip the lamb halfway through.
5. When cooking is done, the lamb should be lightly browned.
6. Now take the lamb and place it on a plate. Brush the fat part with mustard and sprinkle the lamb rack with the pistachios mixture to coat well.
7. Put now the lamb rack back to the air fryer grill and air fry for 8 more min or until the internal temperature of the rack reaches at least 63°C (145°F).
8. Remove the lamb rack from the air fryer grill with tongs and cool for 5 min before slicing to serve.

Nutrition: Calories 200; Fat 12 g; Carbohydrates 8 g; Protein 11 g; Fibre 0 g; Sugar 0.5 g

COTTAGE PIE

| 15 minutes | 40 minutes | 4 |

INGREDIENTS

For the base:
- 300g minced beef
- 4 tbsp onions (coarsely diced)
- 2 tbsp carrots (coarsely diced)
- 4 mushrooms (soaked & diced)
- 4 cloves garlic (minced)
- 1 tsp dried mixed herbs
- 2 bay leaves
- 150 ml beef stock
- 1 tbsp Bovril
- 1 tsp ground black pepper
- 2 tbsp plain flour
- 30g butter

For the potato topping:
- 400g potatoes (quartered)
- 130 ml milk
- 2 tbsp butter
- Pinch of salt

Final egg wash topping:
- 1 egg yolk (beaten)

DIRECTIONS

1. Add 1 teaspoon of salt to a saucepan of water and bring to a boil before adding the potatoes. Cook the potatoes until very tender(15-17 minutes).
2. Melt the butter on the baking tray while preheating the fryer. Everything is prepared on the baking tray at 180 degrees C for this recipe.
3. Fry the onion for 1 minute, then add the garlic and fry for another minute until fragrant.
4. Add the ground beef, carrots, mushrooms, herb mix, black pepper, and bay leaves, mix well and cook for 20 minutes. Stir well every 5 minutes.
5. After 10 minutes, add Bovril and beef broth and stir. Continue stirring every 5 minutes.
6. Sprinkle all-purpose flour into the mixture and mix well 2-3 minutes before the end of the cooking time.
7. Hold the baking tray in the air fryer (to keep it warm) while you mash the potatoes.
8. Add the butter, salt, and milk (a little at a time) to the potatoes, mash, and mix well.
9. Spread mashed potatoes over the meat mixture, leveling with the back of a spoon.
10. Use a fork to draw lines across mashed potatoes, then pour the egg yolk on top.
11. Return the baking tray to the air fryer and cook at 180°C for 20 minutes.
12. Serve warm

Nutrition: Calories 360; Fat 22 g; Protein 19 g; Carbs 20 g; Fibre 2.5 g; Sugar 3 g

CHEESY BEEF MEATBALLS

5 minutes

18 minutes

2-3

INGREDIENTS

- 455 g ground beef
- 65 g grated Parmesan cheese
- 1 tbsp minced garlic
- 65 g Mozzarella cheese
- 1 tsp freshly ground pepper

DIRECTIONS

1. Place the crisper tray on the air fry position. Select Air Fry, set temp to 200°C (400°F) and set the time to 18 min.
2. Get a bowl and combine all the ingredients in it.
3. Roll the meat mixture into 5 meatballs. Transfer to the crisper tray.
4. Air fry for 18 min.
5. Serve immediately.

Nutrition: Calories 176.5; Fat 11.5 g; Carbohydrates 0.2 g; Protein 16.5 g; Fibre 0 g; Sugar 0 g

ROAST BEEF

5 minutes

35 minutes

8

INGREDIENTS

- 1 Kg Beef Roast (up to 1.5 Kg)
- 1 tbsp Olive Oil
- Seasoning to taste

DIRECTIONS

1. Tie the roast to make it more compact
2. Rub the roast with oil
3. Add any seasonings you like
4. Place the beef in the air fryer basket
5. Air fry at 180°C for about 15 minutes per half of Kg (for medium rare beef).
6. Let the roast rest for 5 minutes and serve

Notes

Rare: 46 to 49°C (50 final temperature)

Medium-Rare: 50 to 55°C (58 final temperature)

Medium: 58 to 60°C (63 final temperature)

Medium-Well: 60 to 63°F (65 final temperature)

Well-Done: 65 to 69°F (72 final temperature)

Nutrition: Calories: 443; Fat: 29 g; Carbohydrates: 0 g; Fibre: 0 g; Sugar: 0 g; Protein: 43 g

BEEF WELLINGTON

15 minutes

35 minutes

8

INGREDIENTS

- 1kg beef fillet (one large piece)
- Chicken pate
- 2 sheets of short crust pastry
- 1 egg, beaten
- Salt
- Pepper

DIRECTIONS

1. Season the beef with salt, pepper and wrap tightly in cling film
2. Place the beef in the refrigerator for at least one hour
3. Roll out the pastry and brush the edges with the beaten egg
4. Spread the pate over the pastry, making sure it is distributed equally
5. Take now the beef out of the refrigerator and remove the cling film
6. Place the beef in the middle of your pastry
7. Wrap your pastry around the meat and seal the edges with a fork
8. Place in the Air Fryer and cook at 160°C for 35 minutes

Nutrition: Calories: 509; Fat: 28 g; Protein: 34 g; Carbs: 28 g; Fibre: 1 g; Sugar: 0.5 g

BEEF KEBOBS

45 minutes

15 minutes

5

INGREDIENTS

- 500g beef, cubed
- 200g low fat sour cream
- 2 tbsp. soy sauce
- 1 bell pepper
- ½ onion, chopped
- 20 x 16 cm skewers

DIRECTIONS

1. Take a medium bowl and combine the sour cream and soy sauce
2. Add the cubed beef and marinate for at least 30 minutes
3. Cut the pepper and onion into 2.5 cm pieces
4. Soak the skewers in warm water for about 10 minutes
5. Place the beef, bell peppers and onion onto the skewers, alternating between each one
6. Cook at 200°C for 10 minutes, flip halfway through.

Nutrition: Calories: 250; Fat: 15 g; Protein: 23g; Carbs: 4 g; Fibre: 0 g; Sugar: 0 g

GARLIC BUTTER LOBSTER TAILS

15 minutes

8 minutes

2

INGREDIENTS

- 2 lobster tails
- 2 cloves garlic, minced
- 2 tbsp butter
- 1 tsp lemon juice
- 1 tsp chopped chives
- Salt to taste

DIRECTIONS

1. Butterfly the lobster tails.
2. Place now the meat on top of the shell.
3. Mix the remaining ingredients in a bowl.
4. Add lobster tails inside the air fryer.
5. Set it to air fry.
6. Spread garlic butter on the meat.
7. Cook at 195°C (380°F) for 5 min.
8. Spread more butter on top.
9. Cook for another 2 to 3 min.

Serving Suggestions: Garnish with chopped chives.

Prep & Cooking Tips: You can use frozen lobster tails for this recipe but extend cooking time to 12 min.

Nutrition: Calories 217; Fat 12.5 g; Carbohydrates 0 g; Protein 24.5 g; Fibre 0 g; Sugar 0 g

TERIYAKI SALMON WITH BOK CHOY

 15 minutes

 15 minutes

 4

INGREDIENTS

- 95 g Teriyaki sauce, divided
- 4 (170-g) skinless salmon fillets
- 4 heads baby bok choy, ends trimmed off and cut in half lengthwise through the root
- 1 tsp sesame oil
- 1 tbsp vegetable oil
- 1 tbsp toasted sesame seeds

DIRECTIONS

1. Set aside 30 g of Teriyaki sauce and pour the remaining sauce into a resealable plastic bag. Put the salmon into the bag and seal, squeezing out as much air as possible. Allow the salmon to marinate for at least 10 min.
2. Arrange the bok choy halves on the sheet pan. Drizzle the oils over the vegetables, tossing to coat. Drizzle about 1 tbsp of the reserved Teriyaki sauce over the bok choy, then push them to the sides of the sheet pan.
3. Put now salmon fillets in the middle of the sheet pan.
4. Place the pan on the toast position.
5. Select Toast, set temperature to 190°C (375°F), and set time to 15 min.
6. When done, remove the pan and brush the salmon with the remaining Teriyaki sauce. Serve garnished with sesame seeds.

Nutrition: Calories 253; Fat 11 g; Carbohydrates 2 g; Protein 34 g; Fibre 2.5 g; Sugar 2 g

TILAPIA TACOS

10 minutes

10-15 minutes

6

INGREDIENTS

- 1 tbsp avocado oil
- 1 tbsp Cajun seasoning
- 4 (140 to 170 g) tilapia fillets
- 1 (400-g) package coleslaw mix
- 12 corn tortillas
- 2 limes, cut into wedges

DIRECTIONS

1. Line a baking pan with parchment paper.
2. In a shallow bowl, stir together the avocado oil and Cajun seasoning to make a marinade. Place the tilapia fillets into the bowl, turning to coat evenly.
3. Put the fillets in the baking pan in a single layer.
4. Slide the pan into the air fryer grill.
5. Select Air Fry, set the temperature to 190°C (375°F), and set time to 10 min.
6. When cooked, the fish should be flaky. If necessary, continue cooking for 5 min more. Remove the fish from the air fryer grill to a plate.
7. Assemble the tacos: Spoon some coleslaw mix into each tortilla and top each with 1/3 of a tilapia fillet. Squeeze lime juice over the top of each taco and serve immediately.

Nutrition: Calories 520; Fat 18 g; Carbohydrates 57 g; Protein 31 g; Fibre 4.5 g; Sugar 11.5 g

FAST BACON-WRAPPED SCALLOPS

5 minutes

15 minutes

4

INGREDIENTS

- 8 slices bacon, cut in half
- 16 sea scallops, patted dry
- Cooking Spray
- Salt, freshly ground black pepper, to taste
- 16 toothpicks, soaked for at least 30 min

DIRECTIONS

1. On a clean work surface, wrap half of a slice of bacon around each scallop and secure with a toothpick.
2. Lay the bacon-wrapped scallops in the air fry basket in a single layer.
3. Spritz the scallops with cooking spray and sprinkle the salt and pepper to season.
4. Place the basket on the air fry position.
5. Select Air Fry, set the temperature to 190°C (370°F), and set the time to 10 min. Flip now scallops halfway through the cooking time.
6. When cooking is done, bacon should be cooked through, and the scallops should be firm. Remove the scallops from the air fryer grill to a plate Serve warm.

Nutrition: Calories 125.5; Fat 8 g; Carbohydrates 4 g; Protein 9 g; Fibre 1 g; Sugar 3 g

FISH AND CHIPS

8 minutes

12 minutes

2

INGREDIENTS

- 130 g all-purpose flour, divided
- 1 tbsp corn-starch
- 1/4 tsp baking soda
- 80 ml room temperature beer or water
- 1 egg
- 1/2 tsp salt
- 1/2 tsp black pepper
- 1/2 tsp paprika
- 1/4 tsp garlic powder
- 340 g cod filets, thawed
- Cooking spray

DIRECTIONS

1. Preheat air fryer to 200 C, air fryer setting. In a medium bowl, whisk together half the flour, cornstarch, baking soda, beer or water, and egg until smooth. Set aside.
2. Whisk together the remaining flour, salt, black pepper, paprika, and garlic powder in another medium bowl.
3. Dip the cod, piece by piece, into the batter. Drain excess and coat in the flour mixture. Spray the air fryer basket well with cooking spray or use a piece of parchment paper. Place the fish in the basket, ensuring the pieces don't touch each other.
4. Spray the fish too with a little of cooking spray.
5. Air fry for 10 to 12 minutes at 200 C . Halfway through cooking, spray again with more cooking spray. Turning is not necessary. It's ready when the fish is golden.
6. Sprinkle with a bit of salt if you like.
7. Arrange, serve and enjoy! You can serve with French fries, lemon wedges and tartar sauce for dipping.

Nutrition: Calories 417; Fat 4 g; Carbohydrates 52 g; Protein 40 g; Fibre 2 g; Sugar 1 g

CRAB CAKES

20 minutes

15 minutes

4

INGREDIENTS

For The Crab Cakes:

- Cooking spray
- Hot sauce, for serving
- Lemon wedges, for serving
- 60 g of mayonnaise
- 1 egg
- 2 tsp. of cajun seasoning
- 1 tsp. of lemon zest
- 1/2 tsp. of salt
- 450 g of jumbo lump crab meat
- 120 g of Cracker crumbs (from about 20 crackers)
- 2 tbsp. of chives, finely chopped
- 2 tsp. of Dijon mustard

For The Tartar Sauce:

- 1/4 tsp. of Dijon mustard
- 1 tsp. of fresh dill, finely chopped
- 60 g of mayonnaise
- 80 g dill pickle, finely chopped
- 2 tsp. of capers, finely chopped
- 1 tsp. of fresh lemon juice
- 1 tbsp. of shallot, finely chopped

DIRECTIONS

1. Take a large bowl, whisk together egg, mayo, chives, Dijon mustard, lemon zest, cajun seasoning, and salt. Fold in crab meat and cracker crumbs.
2. Divide your mixture to form 8 patties.
3. Heat your Air Fryer to 190°C, spray the basket and the tops of your cakes with some cooking spray. Arrange the cakes into the basket in a single layer. Cook until crisp and deep golden brown, 12-14 minutes, flip halfway through.
4. Take a bowl and mix all of the tartar sauce ingredients.
5. Serve the cakes warm with lemon wedges, hot sauce and tartar sauce.

Nutrition: Calories: 265; Fat: 8 g; Protein: 24.5 g; Carbs: 21 g; Fibre: 1 g; Sugar: 0 g

TUNA PATTIES

9 minutes   15 minutes   10

INGREDIENTS

- 425 g canned albacore tuna , drained or 454g fresh tuna, diced
- 2-3 large eggs
- zest of 1 medium lemon
- 1 tbsp. lemon juice
- 1/4 tsp of **Kosher salt** , or to taste
- 55 g of bread crumbs
- 1/2 tsp dried herbs (oregano, dill, basil, thyme or any combo)
- fresh cracked black pepper
- 3 tbsp grated parmesan cheese
- 1 stalk celery , finely chopped
- *Optional: tarter sauce, ranch, mayo, lemon slices*
- 3 tbsp minced onion
- 1/2 tsp garlic powder

DIRECTIONS

1. Take a medium bowl, mix the lemon zest, eggs, lemon juice, breadcrumbs, celery, parmesan cheese, onion, dried herbs, garlic powder, salt, pepper. Now stir well. Gently fold in the tuna.
2. Take your Air Fryer perforated baking paper, lay it inside the base of the Air Fryer. Now lightly spray the paper.
3. Try to keep all patties same size and thickness. Scoop 1/4 cup of the mixture, shape into patties about 8 cm wide x 1.3 cm thick and lay them inside the basket. Makes about 10 patties.
4. If patties are too soft, chill them for 1 hour or until firm. Brush the top of the patties with oil. Air Fry 185°C, 10 minutes, flip halfway through. After you flip the patties, spray the tops again.
5. Serve with your sauce and lemon slices.

Nutrition: Calories: 102.2; Fat: 3.9 g; Protein: 12.5 g; Carbs: 2.7 g; Fibre: 0 g; Sugar: 0 g

SIMPLE SALMON

5 minutes

20-25 minutes

4

INGREDIENTS

- 4 salmon filets
- 3 lemons
- 8 sprigs rosemary
- 1 Tablespoon olive oil
- Salt

DIRECTIONS

1 Slice the lemons into thin slices.
2 Place several lemon slices on the bottom of the Air Fryer basket.
3 Now lay 4 rosemary sprigs on the lemons.
4 Arrange one salmon filet on top of each sprig of rosemary. Sprinkle some salt on the salmon.
5 Top each salmon filet with another sprig of rosemary. Cover with more lemon slices.
6 Drizzle with the olive oil on top.
7 Put the fry basket in the fryer. Set the temperature to 135°C. Set the timer for 20 minutes.
8 Take a fork and check the salmon, If it flakes easily, it's ready. If not, it needs 5 minutes more.
9 Serve the salmon with roasted lemon slices and rosemary.

Nutrition: Calories: 242; Fat: 12 g; Protein: 29 g; Carbs: 0 g; Fibre: 0 g; Sugar: 0 g

FRIED BANANAS WITH CHOCOLATE SAUCE

10 minutes

10 minutes

3

INGREDIENTS

- 1 large egg
- 30 g corn flour
- 30 g plain breadcrumbs
- 3 bananas halved crosswise
- Cooking oil
- Chocolate sauce

DIRECTIONS

1. In a small bowl, beat the egg. In another bowl, place the corn flour.
2. Place the breadcrumbs in a third bowl.
3. Dip the bananas in the corn flour, then the egg, and then the breadcrumbs.
4. Spray the air fryer basket with cooking oil. Place the bananas in the basket and spray them with cooking oil.
5. Set temperature to 180°C (360°F) and cook for 5 min. Open the air fryer and flip the bananas—Cook for an additional 2 min. Transfer the bananas to plates.
6. Drizzle the chocolate sauce over the bananas and serve.
7. You can make your chocolate sauce using two tbsp milk and 30 g chocolate chips. Heat a saucepan over medium-high heat. Add the milk and stir for 1 to 2 min. Add the chocolate chips. Stir for 2 min, or until the chocolate has melted.

Nutrition: Calories: 20; Fat: 6g; Protein: 3g; Fibre: 3g

CREAMY CHOCOLATE ECLAIRS

15 minutes   25 minutes   9

INGREDIENTS

Éclair Dough:
- 50 g Butter
- 100 g Plain Flour
- 3 Medium Eggs
- 150 ml Water

Cream Filling:
- 1 tsp. Vanilla Essence
- 1 tsp. Icing Sugar
- 150 ml Whipped Cream

Chocolate Topping:
- 50 g Milk chocolate (chopped into chunks)
- 1 tbsp. Whipped Cream
- 25 g Butter

DIRECTIONS

1. Preheat the Air Fryer to 180°C.
2. While it is heating up, place the butter in the water, melt over medium heat, using a large pan, then bring to the boil.
3. Now remove it from the heat and stir in the flour.
4. Place the pan again to the heat and stir into it forms a medium ball in the middle of the pan.
5. Transfer the dough to a cold plate so that it can cool. Once it is cool beat in the eggs until you have a smooth mixture.
6. Then make into éclair shapes and place in the Air Fryer. Cook for 10 minutes on 180°C and a further 8 minutes on 160°C.
7. While the dough is cooking make your cream filling: Mix with a whisk the whipped cream, vanilla essence and icing sugar until nice and thick.
8. Leave the eclairs to cool and while they are cooling make your chocolate topping - Place the milk chocolate, whipped cream and butter into a glass bowl. Place it over a pan of hot water and mix well until you have melted chocolate.
9. Cover the tops of the eclairs with melted chocolate and then serve!

Nutrition: Calories: 181; Fat: 13 g; Protein: 4 g; Carbs: 27.5 g; Fibre: 1.5 g; Sugar: 3 g

GINGER BISCUITS

10 minutes   16 minutes   10-12

INGREDIENTS

- 270 g plain flour
- 2 tsp ground ginger
- 2 tsp baking soda
- 1 tbsp cinnamon
- ½ tsp salt
- 170 g butter room temperature
- 200 g white sugar
- 1 egg
- 85 g maple syrup
- 70 g sugar for coating the cookies

DIRECTIONS

1. In a large bowl, mix together the flour, ginger, baking soda, cinnamon, and salt.
2. In a second bowl, beat the butter with the sugar, egg, and maple syrup until creamy.
3. Combine the dry ingredients with the wet ones. Once everything is mixed, shape into small balls using your hands.
4. Flat each ball a little (the thicker the better!)
5. Preheat your air fryer at 150°C, and then air fry the cookies for 8 minutes at the same temperature.
6. Add 4-6 biscuits simultaneously (leaving space between each one). It is not necessary to rotate them.
7. Cook until hard on the outside but soft to touch when you press the biscuit.
8. Repeat steps 6-8 for the remaining cookies.
9. Let cool before eating and enjoy!

Nutrition: Calories 300; Fat 14 g; Protein 4 g; Carbs 45 g; Fibre 3 g; Sugar 25 g

CHOCOLATE-COCONUT CAKE

5 minutes

15 minutes

10

INGREDIENTS

- 160 g unsweetened bakers' chocolate
- 1 stick butter
- 1 tsp liquid stevia
- 42.5 g shredded coconut
- 2 tbsp coconut milk
- 2 eggs, beaten
- Cooking Spray

DIRECTIONS

1. Lightly spritz a baking pan with cooking spray.
2. Place the butter, chocolate, and stevia in a microwave-safe bowl. Microwave for about 30 seconds until melted. Let now the chocolate mixture cool down to room temperature.
3. Add the remaining ingredients to the chocolate mixture and stir until well incorporated. Pour now the batter into the prepared pan.
4. Place the pan in the bake position.
5. Select Bake, set temperature to 165°C (330°F), and set time to 15 min.
6. When cooking is complete, a toothpick inserted in the centre should come out clean.
7. Remove from the air fryer grill and allow to cool for about 10 min before serving.

Nutrition: Calories 111.5; Fat 11 g; Carbohydrates 1.8 g; Protein 1.3 g; Fibre 0.1 g; Sugar 1.7 g

CHOCOLATE AND CHILLI BROWNIES IN THE AIRFRYER

15 minutes | 40 minutes | 6

INGREDIENTS

- 200 g butter, melted
- 100 g cocoa powder
- 75 g dark chocolate, melted
- 2 large eggs
- 150 g caster sugar
- 1/2 tsp vanilla essence
- 150 g self-raising flour
- 1 level tbsp crushed dried chilli flakes

DIRECTIONS

1. Preheat the air fryer to 180°C
2. Mix the butter, sugar and crushed dried chillies.
3. Beat and mix in the eggs. Add the melted chocolate and vanilla essence.
4. Gradually add the flour and cocoa powder. Mix gently, do not stir too much.
5. Using a greased or baking paper lined tin/container, pour in the mixture.
6. Cook in the air fryer for 15 to 20 minutes, checking periodically to see if the upper part does not burn; If it's cooking quickly, cover it with foil or baking paper.
7. When it's done, let it cool, then cut into smaller portions to serve.

Nutrition: Calories: 300; Fat: 22 g; Protein: 5 g; Carbs: 19 g; Fibre: 5 g; Sugar: 11 g

FLUFFY BLUEBERRY FRITTERS

5 minutes

15 minutes

4

INGREDIENTS

- 95 g all-purpose flour
- 1 tsp baking powder
- 65 ml coconut milk
- 2 tbsp coconut sugar
- A pinch of sea salt
- 1 egg
- 2 tbsp melted butter
- 55 g fresh blueberries

DIRECTIONS

1. In a mixing bowl, thoroughly mix all the ingredients.
2. Drop a spoonful of batter onto a greased Air Fryer pan. Cook in the preheated Air Fryer at 182°C (360°F) for 10 min, flipping halfway through the cooking time.
3. Repeat now with remaining batter and serve warm. Enjoy!

Nutrition: Calories: 195; Fat 8g; Carbs 25.4g; Protein 4.9 g; Sugars 6.9g; Fibre 1g

CHOCOLATE CHIP COOKIES

10 minutes

8 minutes

12

INGREDIENTS

- 115 g butter, melted
- 55 g brown sugar
- 50 g caster sugar
- 1 large egg
- 1 tsp. pure vanilla extract
- 185 g plain flour
- 1/2 tsp. bicarbonate of soda
- 1/2 tsp. salt
- 120 g chocolate chips
- 35 g chopped walnuts

DIRECTIONS

1. In a medium bowl, combine melted butter and sugar. Add the egg and vanilla and beat until incorporated. Add the flour, baking soda, and salt and stir until combined.
2. Place a small piece of parchment in the frying basket, making sure there is room around the edges to allow air circulation. Working in batches, using a large cookie scoop (about 3 tablespoons), scoop the batter onto parchment paper, leaving 5 cm between each cookie. Press down the batter until slightly flattened.
3. Air fry for 8 minutes at 180 °C. The cookies will turn golden brown and slightly soft.
4. Let cool for 5 minutes before serving.

Nutrition: Calories: 220; Fat: 12 g; Protein: 3 g; Carbs: 24 g; Fibre: 2.5 g; Sugar: 11 g

SHORTBREAD CHOCOLATE BALLS

4 minutes

13 minutes

9

INGREDIENTS

- 175 g Butter
- 75 g Caster Sugar
- 250 g Plain Flour
- 1 tsp. Vanilla Essence
- 9 Chocolate chunks
- 2 tbsp. Cocoa

DIRECTIONS

1. Preheat your Air Fryer to 180°C.
2. Take a bowl and mix your sugar, flour, and cocoa.
3. Rub in the butter, knead well until you see a smooth dough.
4. Now divide into balls, place a chunk of chocolate into the centre of each one, make sure none of the chocolate chunk is showing.
5. Place your chocolate shortbread balls onto a baking sheet in your Air Fryer. Cook them at 180°C for 8 minutes and then a further 5 minutes on 160°C so that you can make sure they are cooked in the middle.
6. Serve!

Nutrition: Calories: 297; Fat: 18 g; Protein: 4 g; Carbs: 31 g; Fibre: 3.5 g; Sugar: 10 g

APRICOT AND RAISIN CAKE

10 minutes

12 minutes

8

INGREDIENTS

- 75g dried apricots, (just under 1/2 cup)
- 4 tbsp orange juice
- 75g self-raising flour, (3/4 cup)
- 40 g Sugar, (1/3 cup)
- 1 egg
- 75g Raisins, (just under 1/2 a cup)

DIRECTIONS

1. Preheat air fryer to 160°C
2. In a blender or food processor, puree the dried apricots and juices until smooth.
3. Put sugar and cake flour in another bowl and mix. Add a beaten egg to flour and sugar and mix together. Add apricot puree and raisins and keep mixing.
4. Spray a small amount of oil on a baking pan suitable for the air fryers. Transfer and flatten the mixture in it.
5. Cook in the air fryer for 12 minutes and check after 10 minutes. Use a metal skewer to check if it is done. If desired, return the cake to the air fryer and brown for a few more minutes.
6. Allow to cool, then remove from pan and slice.

Nutrition: Calories: 116; Fat: 1 g; Carbohydrates: 26 g; Fibre: 1 g; Sugar: 16 g; Protein: 2 g

MINI APPLE PIE

5 minutes

18 minutes

9

INGREDIENTS

- 75 g Plain Flour
- 33 g Butter
- 15 g Caster Sugar
- Water
- 2 Medium Red Apples
- Pinch Cinnamon
- Pinch Caster Sugar

DIRECTIONS

1. Preheat your Air Fryer to 180°C.
2. Start by making your pastry - place the plain flour and butter in a mixing bowl and rub the fat into the flour. Add the sugar and mix well. Add the water until the ingredients are moist enough to combine into a nice dough. Knead the dough well until it has a smooth texture.
3. Cover your pastry tins with butter to stop it sticking and then roll out the pastry and fill your pastry tins.
4. Peel, dice your apples, place in the tins. Sprinkle them with sugar and cinnamon.
5. Add an extra pastry layer to the top and make some fork markings so that they can breathe.
6. Cook in the Air Fryer for 18 minutes.

Nutrition: Calories: 85; Fat: 3 g; Protein: 1 g; Carbs: 13.5 g; Fibre: 1.5 g; Sugar: 6.5 g

INDEX

CREDITS

Icon made by Pixel perfect from www.flaticon.com

Printed in Great Britain
by Amazon

86432339R00045